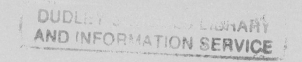
DUDLEY SCHOOLS LIBRARY
AND INFORMATION SERVICE

KU-213-446

Schools Library and Infomation Services

S00000691868

Stay Safe!

Home Safety

Sue Barraclough

www.heinemann.co.uk/library
Visit our website to find out more information about Heinemann Library books.

To order:
☎ Phone 44 (0) 1865 888066
▤ Send a fax to 44 (0) 1865 314091
▯ Visit the Heinemann Bookshop at www.heinemann.co.uk/library to browse our catalogue and order online.

First published in Great Britain by Heinemann Library,
Halley Court, Jordan Hill, Oxford OX2 8EJ, part of Harcourt Education. Heinemann is a registered trademark of Harcourt Education Ltd.

© Harcourt Education Ltd 2008
The moral right of the proprietor has been asserted.

All rights reserved. No part of this publication may be reproduced, stored in a retrieval system, or transmitted in any form or by any means, electronic, mechanical, photocopying, recording, or otherwise, without either the prior written permission of the publishers or a licence permitting restricted copying in the United Kingdom issued by the Copyright Licensing Agency Ltd, 90 Tottenham Court Road, London W1T 4LP (www.cla.co.uk).

Editorial: Diyan Leake and Cassie Mayer
Design: Joanna Hinton-Malivoire
Illustration: Paula Knight
Picture research: Erica Martin
Production: Duncan Gilbert

Origination by Chroma Graphics (Overseas) Ltd
Printed and bound in China by South China Printing Co. Ltd

ISBN 978 0 431 18432 6
12 11 10 09 08
10 9 8 7 6 5 4 3 2 1

British Library Cataloguing in Publication Data
Barraclough, Sue
  Home safety. - (Stay safe!)
  1. Home accidents - Prevention - Juvenile literature
  2. Safety education - Juvenile literature
  I. Title
  363.1'3

Acknowledgements
The publishers would like to thank Robin Wilcox for assistance in the preparation of this book.

Every effort has been made to contact copyright holders of any material reproduced in this book. Any omissions will be rectified in subsequent printings if notice is given to the publishers.

DUDLEY PUBLIC LIBRARIES

L

691868   5CH

J 614 S

Contents

Home is the place where you live.

Do you know how to stay safe
at home?

Never use sharp things.

Always ask a grown-up to help you.

Never play with doors.

Doors can trap your fingers.

Always ask a grown-up to help you reach things.

Never play on the stairs.

Always remember hot things
like fires, heaters, or cookers can
burn you.

Never take medicines on your own.
Some things might make you ill.

Never open bottles or jars.
Always ask a grown-up to help you.

Never leave things on the floor.
People can trip over them.

Always put things away.

Never touch tools or machines.
They can be very dangerous.

Always play far away from tools
and machines.

Never touch wires and plugs.
They are very dangerous.

Always ask a grown-up to switch
something on.

Always remember these safety rules.

Always take care at home and you will stay safe.

Home safety rules

- Ask an adult to help you with sharp things.
- Do not play with doors.
- Ask an adult to help you reach up to things.
- Be careful on stairs.
- Remember that hot things can burn you.
- Ask an adult to help you with bottles.
- Put things away so you do not trip over them.
- Ask an adult to use tools and machines.
- Ask an adult to switch things on.

Picture glossary

 **machine** something that helps people do a job more easily

 **plug** something that goes into a socket to make a machine work

 **switch** turn power on or off

Index

Notes for parents and teachers

Before reading

Talk about things that are dangerous in the home. What things are they told not to touch? Which room do they think is the most dangerous? Tell them that more accidents happen in the kitchen than anywhere else.

After reading

Kim's game. Place the following items on a table and talk about why each one could be dangerous: knife, tin, jar, medicine, drill, saucepan, toaster. Cover the items with a cloth and remove one of them. Display the items again and ask the children what is missing.

Safety game. Make a game board with a path divided into squares. Draw or paste pictures of potentially dangerous items in alternate squares. The children roll a dice and move that number of squares. If they land on a picture and can say how that item can be made safe, they can move forward an extra space – for example, if they land on a picture of matches and say, "Ask an adult to light matches." The winner is the first to get to the end.